BACK IN THE RAIN

The making, unmaking
and remaking of
Bob Dylan's *Blood On The Tracks*

Doc Pasquale

CONTENTS

Introduction:
Back in the Rain

First, there's this cover. This picture like nothing you've seen before. Before, on all those other albums, he turned his face to you, aimed his blue gaze out at you. Here, he's caught in a hunted mugshot profile, eyes shielded by sunglasses that look less like sunglasses than a black wound, eaten halfway into his skull.

But that's not it. What haunts you about this picture is how it seems to be dissolving as you look. It's difficult at first to say whether it's a painting, some unfinished pointillist portrait, abandoned and left to bleed in a rainstorm, or a photograph, shot from a far distance, enlarged till it teeters on the verge of abstraction, the very grain of the air rendered visible. Like the pictures the photographer obsessively amplified in *Blowup*, searching out a murder.

In either case, the grey air around him is swarming, infused with specks red-black and blue, bruised colours, radiating from him like a dark heat. Down the cover's left-hand side, those colours have fused together into a solid purple field. A hexagram, six white lines straight as guitar strings, scrapes that border. On each line floats a simple word, spelling out the name he gave himself and the name he's given the record this cover protects:

Bob Dylan Blood On The Tracks

How this record sounds will hit you soon enough, and it will keep hitting you. But how it sounds is already resounding through the blood and tracks of those words, already bleeding into this picture. Look once more. He seems way out in the distance, yet painfully close. Locked in tight, but out of range. Melting into air, atomising. He seems to be coming apart.

††††††††

Nothing is better, nothing is best, but forty years on from its release in January, 1975, you have to admit that all those who claim *Blood On The Tracks* as Bob Dylan's masterpiece at least have a point.

The majestic amphetamine, spite and mercury trilogy of 1965-66 – *Bringing It All Back Home, Highway 61 Revisited, Blonde On Blonde* – remains untouchable as the work whose white-hot brilliance pushed rock 'n' roll into wild, poison new areas. *Blood On The Tracks*, though, while burning throughout, and sometimes blisteringly cold, is eminently touchable.

Made from time, memory and mystery, from hope and longing and the hate that gets tangled up in love, *Blood On The Tracks* paints a storm landscape, complete with the calm that comes before the storm, the saturated silence left by its passing, and the peace rumoured to exist at its eye.

Most usually, too often, it is described as "Dylan's divorce record", "the greatest breakup album of all time." It is indeed an album on which every song is the same song – the song of love that has been lost – and in its howls and sighs of bitterness, regret and betrayal, of tender regard and faith, and in the black jokes lurking within them, there do seem to be caught echoes of the deterioration of the marriage that had sustained and sheltered him for a decade.

Dylan has always taken vehement issue with the notion the album is autobiographical. "I don't write confessional songs," he flatly stated when *Blood On The Tracks* came up during his 1985 interview with Cameron Crowe for the retrospective compilation album, *Biograph*. Lest the issue become clear-cut, though, he had previously — mockingly? — introduced its most famous song, "Tangled Up In Blue," in concert as one that took him "ten years to live and two to write."

To pin *Blood On The Tracks* down to being of and about the foundering of a specific relationship, however, is to limit it, senselessly cage it. If it can be said to be about his marriage, it can equally be said to be about Dylan confronting the hard reality of his past, the pale, fleeing ghost of his future, and the challenges both presented.

The restless black mood that hounded him during its making (and its subsequent unmaking and final remaking, for part of *Blood On The Tracks'* mystique is founded on the fact that Dylan scrapped, then rerecorded half the album shortly before release) was born of a period of not only personal, but creative turmoil.

In the initial rush of his 1960s success, when Dylan felt himself in trouble, he could always write his way out of it, or write it out of him. Since 1967, however, he had been undergoing what he later termed "amnesia" over how to write. *Blood On The Tracks* is the sound of him making himself remember.

In the same way that he once moved music forward by forcing folk into bed with rock, *Blood On The Tracks* pushed forward again, into a new maturity, but a maturity tempered in the fire of his youth. These are songs, not poetry and not literature, and they are utterly dependant on their performance – Dylan's singing here is unequalled almost anywhere in his studio output – and yet, while remaining true to its own form, this is the record that took the rock 'n' roll album to the level of the novel.

For all its intensely intimate focus, it is the size of a continent, tumbling like Jack Kerouac from coast to coast, tip to tail, sea to shining sea, from bare and blossoming countryside to shadowy cities, through places famed and unheard-of, sweeping its emotions from the Great North Woods to San Francisco, from the Grand Coulee Dam to the Capitol, Ashtabula to Delacroix.

None of this, though, is why *Blood On The Tracks* matters, or why it is the Bob Dylan album most likely to be owned by people who don't buy Bob Dylan albums, nor why it is the album whose implications Dylan still explores most probingly to this day. Erected over a deep network of Bible-haunted blues and folk, country, rock and soul, it contains some of the most incisive, carefully wrought songs in the American songbook, yet its importance has less to do with its place in the history of rock 'n 'roll than with its place in personal histories, the experiences the singer is sharing with his listeners, the experiences his listeners add as they take the record inside. And as, sometimes, they seem to be living inside it.

Dylan's personal troubles fed *Blood On The Tracks*, yes. But placed alongside its monumental achievement, they are like grains of sand. In them, *Blood On The Tracks* sees something universal.

The Big Silence:
Bob Dylan's retreat
1966 – 1974

When Dylan entered New York's A&R Studios in the autumn of 1974 to begin his first attempt at recording *Blood On The Tracks*, he was at the end of a year in which his past, his present and his future had slammed together, and sent him reeling.

It had started that January, when, after a retreat of eight years, he'd reunited with his fabled back-up, The Band, to venture out on the road again for the first time since the punishing 1965-66 tour that took them across the face of a hostile world, as Dylan's electric new sound clashed with the preconceptions of his fans.

In the intervening years since that tour, while he thought he was getting on with living a normal life, Dylan had become rock 'n' roll's most famous recluse, and a perplexity to all who wanted him as The Voice of their generation, happy to let the turbulent decade he'd helped define tumble into the confusion of the 1970s without him, his silence broken only by sporadic albums that telegraphed the strange serenity he'd found as a family man.

His long silence commenced with a crash, in July 1966, when he went tumbling famously over the handlebars of his Triumph motorcycle along a country road near his big wooden house in Woodstock, sending rumours of a broken neck and damaged brain into the world, and bringing his headlong charge across the 1960s to a sudden, deliciously metaphorical halt.

During his subsequent period of recuperation and reflection, the silence spread. It surrounded the whispers of the hundreds of arcane recordings Dylan had made with The Band in mysterious Woodstock basements, yet stubbornly suppressed from release. Then it intensified, into the spartan sound of his first official "post-crash" release, *John Wesley Harding*.

While Dylan removed himself from the scene, the other heads of the 1960s trinity, The Beatles and The Rolling Stones, had chased one another into the chaos territory opened by his long-form mid-60s songwriting, to come up in 1967 with their "psychedelic" epics, *Sergeant Pepper's Lonely Hearts Club Band* and *Their Satanic Majesties Request*, setting off a dippy goldrush as bands tripped to experiment with the possibilities of studio technology.

Cut in three short sessions with seasoned Nashville sidemen, *John Wesley Harding*, released December 1967, seemed a stern rebuke to the cluttered gimmickry of all the acid opuses around it. A cycle of short, stark songs steeped in the Bible, the frontier, and the outlaw balladry of Dylan's first great songwriting model, Woody Guthrie, it was a record that stood outside of time.

Addled fans searching for Dylan's "message" would find the faces of The Beatles hiding in the trees of the cryptic cover photograph, but *John Wesley Harding* was austerely unconcerned with competing as a soundtrack to the Summer of Love, troubled by more lasting matters. While the other pop gurus chased white noise, white rabbits and cellophane taxis, Dylan's comeback dealt in immigrants, messengers and saints. Gnomic, deceptively simple parables, the songs had the sense, as Dylan put it in his 1978

Rolling Stone interview with Jonathan Cott, "of dealing with the Devil in a fearful way."

Or, at least, most of them did. With the final two tracks, "Down Along the Cove," and "I'll Be Your Baby Tonight," the album's mood of lowering dread and mystery lifted curiously, to be replaced by the warm, clear light of oldtime love. The difference between these songs and the others was no coincidence, but neither was it fully deliberate.

In the past, at the peak of his mid-60s rush, most notably while making *Blonde On Blonde*, Dylan had composed almost spontaneously, writing while he was in the studio recording. The songs continued to pour from him in similar improvisatory fashion in his immediate "post-crash" period. The most haunting song he cut with The Band on what came to be called *The Basement Tapes*, the fragmentary lament "I'm Not There (1956)," was one

Dylan was creating even as he sang it, pulling fugitive words and melody half-formed from the air.

In contrast, though, he'd laboured long and hard in his Woodstock study at honing the bulk of *John Wesley Harding*'s lyrics as deliberate texts before he ever thought about putting them to music. But when he'd finished, and looked over what he'd written, Dylan discovered he had become a mystery to himself.

"I didn't know what to make of [that record]," he recalled for Cameron Crowe in 1985. "I figured the best thing to do would be to put it out as quickly as possible, call it *John Wesley Harding*, because that was one song that I had no idea what it was about."

Mystified by his new songs, Dylan then also found himself unable to create in quite the spontaneous manner he had before. Recorded at the end of the sessions, "Down Along the Cove" and

"I'll Be Your Baby Tonight" were, he said, "the only two songs... which came at the same time as the music," but they were markedly unlike the songs he'd previously created this way.

Suddenly gone were what Allen Ginsberg once characterised as the "chains of flashing images," the uncoiling interior impressionism. In their place, moon-spoon rhymes, a sprightly country lilt, and a desire to rhapsodise such mom-and-pop fundamentals as holding hands and seeing your *little bundle of joy*." But while it might not have seemed immediately obvious, for anyone seeking a message, for the next few years, these two songs were it.

"I won't be giving any concerts for a while," Dylan told the world via *Newsweek* magazine upon *John Wesley Harding*'s release. "I'm not compelled to do it now. I went around the world a couple of times.

But I didn't have anything else to do then." And so his silence solidified.

††††††

The other thing he had to do now was get on with raising a family, settling further into the contentment he'd found with Sara, the mystical wife in whose dark eyes he'd found sadness, and in whose name he traced the outline of the Lowlands.

She was married to magazine photographer Hans Lownds when they first met, soon to be divorced. Born Shirley Noznisky, she had been a Bunny Girl at the Playboy Club, a model, a film-production secretary and a mother – her daughter Maria was born in 1961 – before Dylan met her in 1964, while he was conducting his brief, on-off, mostly off, relationship with Joan Baez.

Even though she'd once worn ears and a fluffy tail and he'd first encountered her on the Village scene, Sara, whose inclinations tended toward Eastern philosophies, had no particular interest in a rock 'n' roll lifestyle, nor in the obvious trappings of celebrity. With her striking pale beauty and calm black gaze, her Zen-like detachment from the swirl around her was noted by many, and eulogised repeatedly by Dylan in song, from "She Belongs to Me" to the hymnal "Sad-Eyed Lady of the Lowlands" itself.

He was soon alternating the glamorous, clamorous pressures of his mid-60s existence with quiet days with Sara and her child in the Chelsea Hotel. In 1966, from the centre of the vortex of his world tour and far from home, he'd cast his mind out to her, describing her to biographer Robert Shelton, while they sat high on a plane between gigs, as "holy...

crossing all boundaries of time and usefulness... 'madonna-like.'"

Having bought their Woodstock mansion and married in 1965, when Dylan was in the middle of the methamphetamine-fuelled burst that saw him record three of the greatest albums in rock 'n' roll history and tour the world all in the space of 18 months, his post-accident convalescence was the first chance the couple had to truly experience their marriage. And Dylan took to domesticity with the same evangelical zeal with which he'd once embraced folk and electricity. Sheltered away behind the shushing trees of their property on Camelot Road, they had four children in as many years - Jesse, born 1966, Anna (1967), Samuel (1968), and Jakob (1969) - in addition to Maria, whom Dylan would adopt in 1968, when she was seven.

As that year wore on, between sitting at his piano, devouring almost any book he could lay hands on, and watching his growing babies totter around the wooden floors, Dylan constructed a routine from such things as walking Maria along the leafy lane to her school bus in the mornings, riding his bike, driving his car, walking his dogs through the fields, seeing a few old friends and playing pool.

Striking up a friendship with a close neighbour, Bruce Dorfman, an artist, he developed a serious interest in painting, and asked Dorfman to help him learn to use the set of oils Sara bought him that summer, for his 27th birthday. He spent almost every long and quiet afternoon of the year at Dorfman's studio. "He was a doting parent," Dorfman remembered for Dylan biographer Howard Sounes three decades later. "Loved to talk about his kids... Best thing in the world."

Meanwhile, the world was on fire. In January 1968, the Viet Cong launched the Tet Offensive in South Vietnam.

March saw American troops wreak massacre at Mai Lai. That April, Martin Luther King, at whose side Dylan had stood during "I have a dream," was assassinated in Memphis, inspiring riot in 100 American cities. In May, French students fought the police and tried to burn the Paris Stock Exchange. In June, anti-war Presidential candidate Bobby Kennedy was shot dead in Los Angeles. In August, Chicago briefly became a police state, as the city's force declared war on anti-war demonstrators and waded in. In November, Richard Nixon was sworn in as President.

Even while Dylan was absent, however, he was continually invoked. His words were hurled against the barricades. While their skulls were cracked by nightsticks, the students in Chicago had chanted "the whole world's watching," a phrase manifested from memories of

"When the Ship Comes In," Dylan's 1963 song about slaying "new Goliaths."

As things grew darker in 1969, and hardcore student radicals disappeared underground to unleash a terrorist campaign against the system, they took their battlecry from his "Subterranean Homesick Blues," naming themselves The Weathermen.

All the more shocking to his core audience, then, that when Dylan finally chose to return to the fray that spring of 1969, it was with the pure country *Nashville Skyline* album.

Wrapped in a cover that cast him as happy, hat-doffing Howdy Doody, this was the sound from behind the trees, resolutely deepening the rural furrow he'd started ploughing on *John Wesley Harding*. With the cover's shucksy grin matched by literal exclamations of *"by golly!"* these were songs by a man whose focus had narrowed to celebrating the simple pleasures of feeling the dirt between your toes, of staying put and being alone with the ones you love.

The album soared to number three on the American charts, but out in the campuses and coffeehouses where fans met and muttered, for neither the first nor last time in Dylan's career, feelings of something like betrayal began to grow. It wasn't that he wasn't writing specifically about the seismic events underway; he'd given up "finger-pointing" songs long before. But his mid-60's masterpieces had provided rallying slogans for those who needed them – hippies shovelled *"Something is happening here, but you don't know what it is, do you Mr Jones?"* into the generation gap, without pausing to consider they might be Joneses themselves – and helped chart a newly shattered inner space, mapping the ambiguous psychological landscapes of the era: *"We sit here stranded, though we're all doing our best to deny it."*

Now, though, here he was yelping, *"Oh me, oh my, love that country pie."* Never mind that Dylan had never made any secret of his deep love of the music (*"An' my first idol was Hank Williams,"* he'd declared in his 1963 sleevenotes for *Joan Baez In Concert, Part 2*) in 1969, while America's counterculture hoisted rock as its electric flag, country music was regarded as, precisely, the music of reaction. The same year Merle Haggard had a massive number one with his parodic anti-hippie redneck anthem, Dylan was speaking the language of "The Okie From Muskogee." Soothed by briefly giving up cigarettes, even his voice sounded different, transformed from the old sandpaper and glue into a mellow, plum-coloured croon.

Yet while his thoughts, lifestyle and interests moved further and further from theirs, Dylan remained a fullblown obsession for fans who wanted him as their grand wizard of freakout. His Woodstock tranquility was repeatedly disturbed as a parade of deluded hippies, yippies and fried heads sought him out, trying to tempt him from his cocoon. By the summer of 1969, shortly before the news broke of the Manson clan's visit to Cielo Drive, it had reached the stage where Dylan was discovering gangs camped out on his lawn, naked strangers in his and Sara's bed, disturbed young intruders stalking their hallways by night.

In response, he took possession of a rifle and kept it by his door. Then he moved his family to the other side of Woodstock, halfway up a mountain, hidden behind acres of private land. Still, the unwanted visits continued. "It was like a wave of insanity breakin' loose around the house night and day," he told *Rolling Stone* in 1984, sounding like he was describing *Night Of The Living Dead*. "You'd come in the house and find people there, people comin' through the woods... They kept comin'."

When the rock festival that would draw another 300,000 potential trespassers was staged nearby, it seemed to Dylan, and probably was, just another attempt to persuade him to come back out and play. "That Woodstock festival was the sum total of all this bullshit. And it seemed to have something to do with *me*, this Woodstock Nation, and everything it represented. So we couldn't *breathe*. I couldn't get any space for myself and my family, and there was no help, nowhere. I got very resentful about the whole thing, and we got outta there."

His decision to get out of town as "Three Days Of Peace And Love" unfolded, to journey instead to the Isle Of Wight Festival – where, clad in an immaculate white suit before a sea of dirty denim, he broke his concert silence with a brief, one-hour set which hardly suggested a man bursting to get back in front of his audience – seemed to many fans, and possibly was, Dylan's way of saying, "Fuck you."

His next album, *Self Portrait*, seemed to confirm it. In retrospect, that much-maligned, carefully-titled magpie collection of covers, country, slush and sketches stands as something akin to a Tin Pan Alley addendum to the fabled *Anthology of American Folk Music*.

There's a deep intrigue to such recordings as Dylan's cartoon-meditative Western haiku, "All the Tired Horses," and the sublime backwoods chime of his cover of "Copper Kettle." At the time, though, all anyone could hear was Bob Dylan warbling "Blue Moon" as though through a throatful of Bing Crosby's own syrup, and duetting with himself on a mercilessly parody of Paul Simon's "The Boxer."

By the time it was released, in June 1970, Dylan, fed up being chased through Woodstock, had retreated with his family back to a brick townhouse in New York. That house, too, was soon besieged by "the Woodstock Nation," in particular the self-styled "garbologist" AJ Weberman. The latter, who'd made it his life's mission to bring Dylan "back" to the counterculture, staged protests in the street outside the singer's front window, and sought to divine the secret state of Dylan's body and soul by sifting through the contents of the family's household garbage, and then publishing his findings.

When Weberman had started going through his trashcans, Dylan responded by filling them with dogshit; eventually, one notorious night, he took to bouncing Weberman's head off the sidewalk. *Self Portrait*, he later claimed, was a similar undertaking, aimed at putting off all who came looking for him to live up to their ideas of who he was. "I said, 'Well, fuck it,'" he maintained in 1984. "'I wish these people would just forget about me. I wanna do something they can't possibly like, they can't relate to.'"

Whether or not this was ever his true intention, it did the trick, as the famous opening sentence of Greil Marcus's *Rolling Stone* review testified: *"What is this shit?"*

When *New Morning* followed just four months later, such was the relief to find Dylan writing again it was received as the great comeback. And, buoyed by the unique, hesitant, then growingly confident sound Dylan makes when he paws and pounds a piano, it was a glowing thing, the sound of summer morning. But still, Dylan's concerns remained the same: being with the one you love, running for the hills.

"Build me a cabin in Utah," he sung contemplatively on the sublime "Sign on the Window", *"Marry me a wife, catch rainbow trout/ Have a bunch of kids who call me Pa / That must be what it's all about."*

The difference now, though, was that, listening to the songs for what they were, rather than what they were not, his audience finally accepted that Dylan had metaphorically gone off to his shack on the mountain. Gone away, gone fishin'. He'd made his bucolic getaway, singing to nobody but himself.

††††††††

And of course, this was exactly what he'd always done: giving voice to his state of mind. "I was changing," Dylan said of the period in a 2004 interview with *The Sunday Telegraph*. "I had a wife and kids and different responsibilities. I realised I had to try to settle for another type of life; to take enjoyment out of little things."

As the equivocation still ringing through that quote – "had to *try* to *settle* for another type of life" – suggests, however, he was growing restless. For all the surface calm of *Nashville Skyline* and *New Morning*, since 1967, Dylan had been undergoing a creative crisis, what he later called his "amnesia."

If it had started the day he read over "John Wesley Harding" to discover he had "no idea what it was about," it had intensified when he found he no longer had access to the well of spontaneous creation from which he'd drawn his greatest 1960s work.

As he described it to Jonathan Cott, "One day I was half-stepping, and the lights went out. And since that point, I more or less had amnesia... It took me a long time to get to do consciously what I used to be able to do unconsciously."

While most songwriters would willingly endure any affliction that could result in "I'll Be Your Baby Tonight", "Lay Lady Lay", "I Threw It All Away", "Tonight I'll Be Staying Here With You," or "Sign on the Window," Dylan had begun to sense he was in a hole. The more he tried to dig himself out, the deeper it grew.

"On *Nashville Skyline*, you had to read between the lines. I was trying to grasp something that would lead me on to where I thought I should be, and it didn't go nowhere — it just went down, down, down. I was convinced I wouldn't do anything else."

One of the few songs he recorded in 1971, the single, "Watching the River Flow," came at the listener with a raucously upbeat thump and thrust; but its opening lines spoke directly from the shaking heart of Dylan's dilemma: *"What's the matter with me?/ I don't have much to say…"*

As his restiveness grew, so his dormant wanderlust began to waken. Dylan began to cast increasingly around for direction: finally publishing his senseless 1965 speed-prose anti-novel, *Tarantula*, in 1970; moving his family again, from New York's goldfishbowl to the beachlands of Malibu, California, in 1971; journeying to Mexico to make his curious acting debut in Sam Peckinpah's *Pat Garrett And Billy The Kid* in 1972; letting his contract with Columbia, the label that had been his home since his first recordings, lapse after he delivered them the Peckinpah movie's soundtrack.

Increasingly, it seemed he was wondering whether the way ahead might not be the way back, back to the stage. In the summer of 1971, George Harrison prevailed upon him to play his benefit for Bangladesh, only Dylan's third appearance on an American stage in five years (following performances at 1968's

Woody Guthrie tribute and a spot for The Johnny Cash Show in 1969). The crowd reacted ecstatically to his 20 minute set, particularly as all the songs he played dated from the pre-crash days; especially surprising given that, when Harrison had begged him to play "Blowin' in the Wind," Dylan snapped back, "You gonna sing 'I Wanna Hold Your Hand'?"

Then, that winter, he turned up as a surprise guest at The Band's New Year's show at New York's Academy Of Music, unleashing a performance that recaptured their surging fire of 1966.

Afterwards, Band drummer/ singer Levon Helm asked Dylan the big question point blank:

"When are we gonna go on the road together again?"

On the Road, Off the Road: 1974

The seed planted by Helm that night in New York took root in the summer of 1973, when Band guitarist Robbie Robertson moved out to live near Dylan in Malibu. Robertson had been being enthusiastically courted for a while by David Geffen for his fledgling west coast label, Asylum, and introduced the young entrepreneur to Dylan. At Geffen's insistent urging, Dylan, momentarily without a label, agreed to sign a short-term deal: one studio album for Asylum, and, most significantly, a coast-to-coast megatour with The Band, from which would be culled a live record.

When Geffen talked up this "comeback" tour as "the biggest thing...

in the history of show business," he was not exaggerating by much. Rock 'n' roll's first stadium tour, it saw Dylan's silence ripped apart, transforming him overnight from rock's most famous recluse to the biggest draw on the planet. Over five million people in the USA applied for 650,000 seats. The world's press headed for the opening show at Chicago Stadium to see whether expectations could possibly be met.

Until he stepped out onstage that first night, January 3, 1974, the crowd had barely let itself believe that Dylan – the real Dylan, not one of the "New Dylans" who had sprung up and melted away in his absence – had really returned. When he ripped into a radically rewritten version of 1963's obscure "Hero Blues" – *"One foot on the highway, and one foot in the grave..."* – the audience released eight-years' worth of pent-up frustration in an orgasm *The Guardian*'s reporter described as sounding "like Chicago tearing itself in half."

However, not everyone so welcomed Dylan's return to the road. Inevitably, the near-psychotic attention of fans, which had seen their family chased from coast to coast, had left its mark on his marriage. The rising fitfulness of his peculiar writer's block hadn't helped. During the three hellish months they'd spent in flu-swept Durango while Dylan worked confusedly on the filming of *Pat Garrett*, Sara had made no secret of her disdain for the booze-sodden boys' club Sam Peckinpah presided over. "My wife got fed up almost immediately," Dylan recalled in 1985. "She'd say to me, 'What the hell are we doing here?' It was not an easy question to answer."

It's reasonable to assume his decision to head out along the highway again for a campaign that would take him from her, their children and the new house they'd started building for six weeks, added its extra strain. In that time, Dylan was scheduled to play forty dates in twenty-one cities, by no means a lightweight schedule. Sara had her memories of nursing him through the nastiest days of 1965-66, when he'd kept up with his raging mind and phenomenal workload via a massive intake of Beaujolais, pot, amphetamines and, many speculated, heroin. That regime had left severe dents in his physical and mental make-up at the time: "Takes a lotta medicine to keep up this pace," he'd told Robert Shelton in 1966. "A concert tour like this has almost killed me... I have a death thing, I know... a suicide thing." The spectre that he might succumb to old moods, old ways, old temptations loomed large.

Certainly, the songs Dylan wrote for *Planet Waves*, the Asylum album that accompanied the new tour, spoke of an internal struggle already underway.

Tracks like the rollicking "On A Night Like This," stuck to the now-familiar pastoral family-man groove, warm nights spent locked away in the cabin together, sheltering from the storming snow.

Written for the birth of Jakob, the majestic "Forever Young" – a song Dylan had been labouring over for almost five years, yet which sounded so natural it was as if it had always just existed – was the prayer of a father beseeching the universe to watch over his child. But also the prayer of a man acknowledging he might not be there to do it himself.

The darkness gathered in "Going, Going, Gone," a bleak leavetaking with an air of closed-down finality. The song's narrator is closing the book on a period of his life, not caring what happens next, but knowing something different must: *I been playin' it straight/ Now, I've just got to cut loose..."*

With "Dirge" night came falling down. Often taken as Dylan's comment on his relationship with his audience, really, it's equally plausible as the song of a man lambasting himself, for his slavish dependency on all the things he ever needed: fans, drugs, audience, work, lovers, love, his muse. "I hate myself for loving you." Claimng independence, he burns down the house behind him as he leaves.

Finally, though, with Whitmanesque self-contradiction there is "Wedding Song," which sees Dylan reborn as the solo acoustic troubadour of old, his voice urgent and warm, but stripped bare of its recent mellowness. The song sounds a reaffirmation of total love for the woman who *"gave me babies... saved my life."* Again, though, it's sung by one who has already decided to go, reassuring his love, even as he leaves, that he will return, and not disappear on any crusade: *"It's never been my duty to remake the world at large, nor is it my intention to sound a battle charge";* and by one who views their love itself as a fierce kind of battle, *"eye for eye and tooth for tooth."*

In the space between these final two songs, the song of hate and the song of love, the atmosphere of Dylan's next album began to form.

Meanwhile, out on the road, old temptations came his way. His resubscription to cigarettes and alcohol was the least of it. This was the period when the cocaine blizzard was reaching its initial peak (by 1976, at their farewell concert, The Band would have a backstage "sniffing room"), when the aftershow parties attracted Jack Nicholson, and when there were always girls around. According to Dylan biographer Clinton Heylin, The Band's Richard Manuel instructed the stage crew to collect Polaroids of prospective groupies, so they could be vetted for backstage admittance.

Along the way, Dylan began spending time with Ellen Bernstein, a 24-year-old who happened to work for Columbia, his old label, which, in light of the tour's massive success and *Planet Waves* becoming Dylan's first number one album in America, was keen to get him back into the fold. Actress Ruth Tyrangiel, later to show up in Dylan's movie *Renaldo & Clara* – playing "the girlfriend" – has also claimed she began a long affair with Dylan during the tour.

It was on stage, however, that he was engaged in his most desperate struggle. As captured on the live album, *Before The Flood*, he and The Band were on thunderous form, and were received with nothing but adulation. But Dylan was becoming seriously disturbed by the audiences' thoughtless love. For Robbie Robertson, the shows they were playing now weren't so dissimilar to those they had played in 1966; but where the earlier, epochal concerts had been met with boos and *Judas* cries, in 1974, as Robertson remembered for Howard Souness, "everybody cheered and acted like, '*Oh, I loved it all along.*'"

As far as Dylan was concerned, however, 1966 and 1974 were drastically different affairs. In his uneasiness his thoughts returned repeatedly to the phantom figure of rock 'n' roll's original avatar, Elvis Presley. "When [Elvis] did 'That's All Right, Mama' in 1955, it was sensitivity and power," Dylan said in 1980. "In 1969, it was just full-out power. There was nothing other than force behind that. I've fallen into that trap, too [on the] 1974 tour."

"You could compare [it] to early Elvis and later Elvis, really," he repeated in 1985. "We were cleaning up, but it was an emotionless trip."

For the crowds, though, it was as if the promise of the 1960s was being bottled and sold. While Tour '74 steamrollered across America, Nixon's presidency, crippled by Watergate, was entering its death throes. Each night, as Dylan stood alone to perform 1965's "It's All Right Ma (I'm Only Bleeding)," when he reached its prescient dagger-line about the President of the United States sometimes having to *"stand naked,"* the audience erupted as if on cue, cheering like a pantomime crowd. It seemed they had their Dylan, their spokesman back.

As the tour progressed, the number of post-crash songs dwindled as mid-60s material took dominance. Even as he sang those songs, though, Dylan could barely remember how he'd ever written them. He recognised a condition Rimbaud, the symbolist poet he'd taken as one of his greatest mid-60s influences, had once described: "The poet... losing the understanding of his visions." In 2004, Dylan would recall that, at its worst, the weight of his old songs became like "carrying a package of rotting meat."

By the end of the tour, feeling the chains of the 1960s heavy at his ankles, he was faced with the stark prospect of becoming some nostalgia act for the hordes who held cigarette lighters aloft and swayed to the echoes of yesterday. Of living forever in the shadow of his iconic younger self, as though he'd died in that motorcycle crash, but his body had kept moving.

When Rimbaud had run out of poems as a young man, he'd abandoned writing to take up gun-running and dealing in slaves. Sincerely spooked, Dylan beat another kind of retreat: away from electricity, size and volume, toward older ways, acoustic guitars, and a new aloneness.

†††††††

Tour '74 ended on Valentine's Day in LA. Dylan returned home, more restless than ever — and still in contact with some of the women he'd met on the road. In the following months the cracks started to show in his marriage. By early summer, he and Sara would be living apart.

She'd thrown herself into remodelling their house in Malibu, a project that started as a dream but would spiral out of hand to consume three stressful years. Dylan's most pressing project, meanwhile, was reordering his imagination. On May 24, 1974 he turned 33, entering the perilous limbo of being not yet old, yet no longer quite young. For someone who had made personal icons out of James Dean, Hank Williams, and Jesus Christ, and found in their short lives clues about how to shape his own, it was an age of heavy portent. Dylan had outlived his idols, and he faced his future on his own.

It would be wide of the mark to suggest thoughts of his mortality began to occur to him then. Growing up in Minnesota's bleak Iron Range, he'd clung to Williams's cheerily, desperately lonesome voice on the radiowaves of the pre-rock 'n' roll night, and he had recognised his desolate joke early on: *You'll never get out of this world alive.*

By the time he made his own first recordings, as a puppyfat blues faker of 20, he was already imploring the world to make sure his grave be kept clean, with the ragged urgency of a man facing his own burying ground.

The vital fact of his own finiteness was a key factor in Dylan's abandonment of America's self-styled "folk purist" brigade in the mid-60s, his graduation from writing "protest songs" to writing songs that protested existence itself.

How clear death always was to him seethed to the surface in the extraordinary truth-attack he unleashed on *Time* journalist Horace Judson during his 1965 British tour, immortalised in DA Pennebaker's documentary, *Don't Look Back*. Judson is another of those who comes asking what Dylan's "message" is: "You're gonna die," Dylan says, laying it out flat. "So am I. I mean, we're just gonna be gone. The world's gonna go on without us. Alright now: you do your job in the face of that, and how seriously you take yourself, you decide."

But if Dylan had no mid-life crisis, the thought that he might well have been in the middle of his life must have occurred to him. In the time of his seclusion, he'd lost both Woody Guthrie, the spiritual father to his songwriting, who died October, 1967, aged 55, and, most devastatingly, his own father, Abe

Zimmerman, who passed away in the summer of 1968 aged only 56.

If Dylan had a chronic awareness of life's absurdity and brevity, however, his need to find some balance to it burned just as fiercely. First there had been his work, then the transcendent love he'd found with Sara – *"marry me a wife... raise a bunch of kids... that must be what it's all about."* Now that he was fighting through creative impasse, and the shelter of marriage was beginning to fail him, however, his mind was alert to other answers.

He found one in early spring 1974, when several friends of Sara visited the house. "They were talking about truth and love and beauty and all these words I had heard for years," he told Jonathan Cott in 1978, "and they had 'em all defined. I couldn't believe it... I asked them, 'Where do you come up with all those definitions?' and they told me about this teacher..."

This mysterious guru was one Norman Raeben, whose influence would change Dylan's way of thinking so profoundly it proved the key to unlocking his "amnesia" – while also estranging him further from his wife.

The artist son of Shalom Aleichem, the Ukraine-born Jewish writer beloved as "the Yiddish Mark Twain," Raeben was 73 years old in 1974, and teaching an art class at the Carnegie Hall studios. Seeking him out, Dylan drifted back to New York City, where it had all begun for him over a decade before. He spent two-and-a-half months in the city. By night he could be found haunting clubs and bars he'd first toured in the 1960s, as though trying to pick up the trace of an old scent.

By day, he studied at Carnegie Hall, from 8am till 4pm, Monday to Friday, surrounded by a bizarre cross-section of humanity. Fellow students ranged from struggling and serious young artists to

Florida widows, bus drivers to off-duty cops. Raeben had no interest in Dylan as that public myth "Bob Dylan" – the same quality the singer had treasured in his Woodstock neighbour, Bruce Dorfman, as well as in Sara herself. Indeed, he had no idea who he was at all. Suspecting the scruffily turned-out Dylan a derelict, the old teacher offered to allow him to sleep in the studio, if he'd help with the cleaning.

As he sat drawing and painting through the days, Dylan listened to the old man's incessant discourse. An irascible, multi-lingual guru, as Raeben moved around he'd sometimes explode *"Idiot!"* his favourite word for students who couldn't grasp what he was offering, and a word that lodged in Dylan's mind.

"He would tell me about myself when I was doing something, drawing something," Dylan recalled for journalist Pete Oppel in 1978. "It wasn't art or painting. It was a course in something else. I had met magicians, but this guy is more powerful than any magician I've ever met. He looked into you and told you what you were."

Raeben's main theme with Dylan was a kind of Cubist approach to perspective, to time, to existence itself, the need to develop a vision that was fixed but constantly shifting, until, as Dylan put it, "you've got yesterday, today and tomorrow all in the same room."

It was Raeben, Dylan told Jonathan Cott, who "put my mind and my hand and my eye together, in a way that allowed me to do consciously what I unconsciously felt."

Mind on fire with possibilities, Dylan began to apply Raeben's approach not to his painting, but to his true vocation, suddenly writing songs at a rate he hadn't since 1966. Burning with the zeal of the converted, however, he was heading into areas Sara couldn't follow. "It changed me," he told Pete Oppel. "I went home after that and my wife never did understand me ever since that day. That's when our marriage started breaking up."

Their split widened to a chasm. Dylan moved out. He'd bought a tumbledown farm in Minnesota and, suddenly ejected from the intense intimacy of his nine-year retreat with Sara, he spent the summer of 1974 ensconced there, back under the skies and dragon clouds of his youth, caught in a swamp of time, guilt, bitterness and freedom, and writing furiously.

Ellen Bernstein visited. Dylan's children came, without their mother, but still crying for her. Mainly though, summer passed in the form of mornings spent with his guitar and his notebook, alone in his writing room, looking out over the fields. There were, however, intrusions from the world outside; Dylan was incensed to find reports of his marital difficulties beginning to appear in syndicated gossip columns, even if they wrongly linked him with John Sebastian's ex-wife, Lorey. Dipping his pen into his anger, he kept writing. *"Someone's got it in for me. They're planting stories in the press.."*

By late July, still writing, he felt ready to road test the material, and emerged again, launching a series of intensely private performances. Dylan played a half-dozen of his new songs for Stephen Stills and a stunned Tim Drummond in a hotel room after a Crosby, Stills and Nash show. Showing up at the home of Michael Bloomfield, the guitarist who'd helped him plug into the modernist blues at the Newport Folk Festival in 1965, he charged through the songs with such urgency Bloomfield was left bewildered as he tried to follow on guitar.

As the songs continued to ferment and mutate, further covert, imprompteau concerts followed, in friends' and musicians' homes, including that of the country writer and children's Author Shel Silverstein.

By that September, Dylan was ready to get what had been stewing inside him for five months, for eight years, out and onto vinyl.

In the Studios:
Making Blood On The Tracks.
And Making it Again.

After the long dance with Asylum, Dylan signed back with Columbia again at the start of August. As if to deliberately intensify a sense of time repeating, looping itself around him, he then insisted that the recording of his new record take place at the old Columbia Studio A, where, a lifetime before, he had cut the first six albums that established his myth. The place had since been sold-off and renamed A&R Studios, but Columbia's legendary talent scout John Hammond, the man who'd first signed the young Dylan, booked him sessions there with

Phil Ramone, one of the studio's new owners, engineering.

Ramone found himself with less than a day to round up musicians. He called in Eric Weissberg, the multi-instrumentalist who'd recently had a massive hit with "Duelling Banjos," the rinky-dink tune he'd covered for the movie *Deliverance*. On the back of its success, he'd put together a touring band named after the film: guitarist Charlie Brown; drummer Richard Crooks; bassist Tony Brown; keyboardist Tom McFaul. Their customary work involved recording jingles for radio and TV commercials. Now, on the night of September 16, 1974, they were being called upon to catch lightning as Dylan arrived, reached for a bottle of wine and, with his muse rioting again, proceeded to charge into recording the most complex and confident cycle of songs he'd written since 1967.

As the session began, the musicians were left floundering in his wake. Dylan would run through a song, something infinitely long and twisting, or something brief and elusive, just once, and then ask immediately for the tapes to roll, leaving them to jump in, trying to remember what he'd played, trying to keep up. Their task was made all the more difficult by the fact that, stimulated by the sound of Joni Mitchell's own confessional LP, *Blue*, Dylan was experimenting with the richer, ringing, cosmic tone achieved by open-tuning his guitar, making reading the chords as he formed them almost impossible. Meanwhile, as his mind churned, he rarely played the same thing the same way twice, anyway.

It was a kind of madness, but there was method to it. Having carried these tracks in his head for five months, Dylan was determined to get them down as spontaneously and rawly alive as was still possible. As he battered and caressed his guitar, leaning into the mic, the buttons on his jacket sleeves rattled and clicked a distinctly audible counter-rhythm against the strings, but he didn't pay it any mind. The wine flowed. The band found their groove. By midnight they'd run through 30 perpetually shifting takes.

Dylan, though, was dissatisfied with most of what they'd achieved and resolved to rein the songs back in toward him again. Three more sessions followed, on the nights of the 17th, the 19th and the 24th, for which he asked just Brown, the bass player, to return alone. The first of these, with the two musicians alone in the enormous room at Studio A, became a psychodrama of almost claustrophobic intensity, Dylan barely speaking a word to Brown as he seemed to get lost inside his songs of lost, rejected, demonic and abandoned love. As the night wore itself out, his performance took on a stark nakedness, of sound, and of soul, his focus narrowing to the point where all that existed in the world was each word as he sung it, the pain and wonder of it.

The intensity failed to let up on the 19th, when Dylan called in keyboardist Paul Griffin, a veteran of the *Highway 61 Revisited* album, to provide organ runs that caught the shivering quiet of the Manhattan night. On the 24th, pedal guitarist Buddy Cage was recruited, required by Dylan to overdub on some tracks. Made to record the same part over and over again, without Dylan ever explaining why, Cage finally ripped off a run of almost explosive anger in frustrated retaliation − only for Dylan to tell him that was the sound he'd been waiting for all along.

A number of well-wishers and hangers-on gradually gathered in the production booth, including Mick Jagger who, as his senses disappeared with the wine, begged repeatedly to be allowed to play drums on the album. Dylan passed the offer up. By the time that last night ended, at 3AM, he knew *Blood On The Tracks* didn't need another thing. He'd got it all out, nailed it perfectly.

So then, of course, he decided to rip it up and start again.

††††††

Proud of the public return of their prodigal son, Columbia had planned to have *Blood On The Tracks* on the racks before Christmas 1974. The sleeve design had already been finallised: Dylan himself picked the cover shot, an image of him onstage in Toronto in 1974, which the photographer, Paul Till, had enlarged, solarized and hand-coloured. For the back cover, meanwhile, a sketchy painting by another of Dylan's artist friends, David Oppenheim, was surrounded by a heated, valedictory essay-poem by Pete Hamill, written upon hearing one of the few advance pressings of the album.

A backlog at Columbia's pressing plant, however, had pushed the release date back, until early in 1975. As the months crawled by, Dylan, who'd banked upon the album being out within a few weeks, began to develop serious doubts about the record he had made.

On one level, it was simply another manifestation of his eternal restlessness; these songs never stopped evolving in his head, yet here they were, frozen static on this disc.

Since *John Wesley Harding*, practically every record he had made had been hailed somewhere as some kind of "comeback." With *Blood On The Tracks*, though, for the first time he felt the weight himself. His first statement since the massive success of Tour'74 — and the first since he'd looked into the mirror during that campaign, and saw himself becoming some acid-hipster equivalent to Las Vegas Elvis – this was his chance to finally kick the dust of the 1960s from his heels, establish a new basecamp and strike out for the future on his own terms. The songs, he knew, were strong enough. But the more he listened to these recordings, the greater his dissatisfaction grew.

On another level again, he might have been wondering whether to go back and cover his tracks. Written and recorded amid the immediate fall out of his separation from Sara – with whom a tentative reconciliation was now brewing – there were moments in these songs, lines, words, breaths, that cut deep, and far nearer to the knuckle than he was comfortable with.

Despite his claims to never have written "confessional songs," in 1964, on *Another Side of Bob Dylan*, he'd done just that with "Ballad in Plain D," a song that laid out in no uncertain terms the intimate details of his bitter break up from his first New York girlfriend-muse, Suze Rotolo – and a song that he had regretted writing ever since.

As the Christmas period commenced, Dylan returned to his farm in Minnesota, where his younger brother, David Zimmerman, was also living with his family in an adjoining house. Dylan had with him an acetate test-pressing of the new album. As his doubts grew, he played it for David and asked his opinion.

Five years Dylan's junior, David had grown up sharing with him the usual older-brother-younger-brother baggage of affection, annoyance, rivalry and frustration. When he got his first motorcycle as a James Dean-obsessed teen in 1957, Dylan got his kicks by making his kid sibling stand petrified in the family driveway while he drove the bike straight at him. Time and maturity had evened out their kinship; the two had grown closer than ever following the death of their father.

David had followed Dylan into music, albeit on a far more modest scale, working as a producer in the Minneapolis area, overseeing advertising jingles and a few local singers. With an ear tuned to what went over on the radio, he was struck by the stark, unembellished sound of Dylan's new set. He suggested some tracks might benefit from some fixing up and filling-out. Dylan was uncertain enough to agree.

On Christmas Eve, Dylan made a telephone call to an alarmed Columbia, telling them to halt the production of the album, as he prepared to record it again, pretty much on the spot.

Putting the call out to a group of jobbing and part-time local musicians — bassist Billy Peterson; drummer Bill Berg; keyboardist Gregg Inhofer; guitarists

Kevin Odegard and Chris Webber; and mandolin player Peter Ostroushko – David booked time on the nights of December 27 and 30 at his regular recording venue, Minneapolis' Sound 80 Studios, an anonymous box tucked away in an industrial part of town, near the banks of the Mississippi.

In there, nursing a cold, and with his six-year-old son Jakob in tow, Dylan threw himself into overhauling *Blood On The Tracks*. Gradually interacting far more than he had in New York with the musicians around him, yet striving to maintain a level of spontaneity (some of the recordings that would appear on the album from these sessions were first takes), he was everywhere, restlessly switching instruments, overdubbing sections, and continuing to rewrite songs in the corner of the studio.

Across two whirlwind nights, as 1974 died in the snow outside, he rerecorded

five songs, half the album, and arguably
its key tracks. Within four weeks, the
music world would be reeling from the
results.

Blood on the Tracks
and its Shadow:
Side One

Of all the fables that have grown up around Bob Dylan's many unreleased recordings, none has quite the allure of the legend of *The Two Blood on the Tracks*. It is an article of faith among many obsessives that the album that Dylan officially released is only the shadow of that which he originally recorded across those four nights in New York – and that on those secret, much-bootlegged recordings, he revealed himself like he never had before, or would again.

Like most legends there is some truth about it. Like most legends, it is far from being completely true. Taken individually, those first New York Sessions tracks are magnificent. Listened to together as an album, though, there's a uniformity of sound, rhythm, pace and mood – generally, a kind of regret so tender as to be painful - that becomes mesmerisingly oppressive in a way that the released record, which ranges from regret to utter, stampeding, liberating rage and back, does not.

Proof lies in the first notes of the first track listeners would have heard January 25th, 1975, when they got home from the store and dropped the needle to the record for the first time.

Released in its "Minneapolis version," the opener "Tangled Up in Blue," the first great song unleashed by Dylan's application to Norman Raeben's teaching, is the key to *Blood On The Tracks*, the song that contains all the songs that will follow.

Women, love and, most of all, being adrift in the ocean of time are this album's subjects, and in "Tangled Up in Blue," Dylan establishes all this with his first three words. He begins with a shout from eternity: *"Early one morning..."*

It's a timeless opening, one that echoes back across centuries to touch the ancient English folksong of that title, the ballad whose anonymous narrator is haunted at the rising of the sun by the lament he hears, on the air or in his mind, of a sorrowful maid abandoned by her lover, perhaps him: *"O, don't deceive me/ O, never leave me/ How could you use/ A poor maiden so?"*

Across the album, Dylan narrates this same tale of abandoned love over and over again, playing the lover who gets left, the lover who leaves, and the narrator who records it all from a distance. Sometimes, playing all these figures at once. In "Tangled Up in Blue," the itinerant narrator is hounded from east to west, from one end of history to another, by memories of love, how it went wrong, and his need to find it again.

This is literally a song about seeing, as the lyric states, from different points of view, and in its early, "New York" incarnation, Dylan constantly shifted perspectives, from first-person "I" and "We" to third-person "He" and "They." The album version, however, opts for the immediate (although traces of the methodology still remain, when the narrator recalls living with a couple on *"Montague Street,"* and it gets difficult to say whether he was involved in some menage a trois, or whether that couple was himself and his lover, and that the people they were then are strangers to him now).

In keeping with that first-person approach, the released version, carried on its endless, spangling guitar figure and the intuitive skip and kick of Bill Berg's drumming, has a present-tense drive lacking in its barer, more acquiescent

New York counterpart. Where the New York narrator seems resigned, reflective, the Dylan of Minneapolis is right there, right in the middle of things. The song jump-cuts around him in a blizzard of razor-sharp moments – raindrops hitting shoes, an abandoned car, the side of a woman's face in a spotlight – until time becomes a kaleidoscope, until "you've got yesterday, today and tomorrow all in the same room."

"I wanted to defy time," Dylan stated in 1985, "so that the story took place in the present and the past at the same time. When you look at a painting, you can see any part of it, or see all of it together. I wanted that song to be like a painting."

In accordance with this temporal Cubism, the song's language has no fixed period. The archaic opening and the references to 13th century Italian poets (most likely Dante, who fell in love with his "Beatrice," then lost her to another man, and then to death) sit alongside flip pulp puns and hardboiled lines — *"I had a job in the Great North Woods... but one day the axe just fell"* — that would fit a 1940s film noir, suited to the song's image of outlawed lovers, on the run through the States. As well as recalling Sara, when Dylan writes *"She was married when we first met, soon to be divorced/ I helped her out of a jam I guess, but I used a little too much force..."* it's voiceover dialogue worthy of Dashiell Hammett. (10 years later, Dylan would actually crib dialogue from Hammett's *The Maltese Falcon* for his *Empire Burlesque* album.)

By the end of the song, as the narrator heads off again, still searching for the love he once knew, sometime, but lost, someplace, the language has absorbed post-war hipster phraseology, from Kerouac to Curtis Mayfield; *"on the road, heading for another joint,"* all he knows how to do is *"keep on keeping on."*

It's a quagmire collage. Every moment and meaning stands on others. *"There was music in the cafes at night/ And revolution in the air"* offers the thrill of Dylan sketching a self-portrait of himself moving through the mythic landscape of the New York 1960s; but it also throws out hints of 1917, 1789, 1776. Something dies inside a man, and he turns into the burnt-out Rimbaud and starts *"dealing in slaves."*

The narrator is uneasy when he meets the woman who hands him Italian poetry, because she bends to tie his shoes. Is it because her movement recalls a mother tending to her helpless child? Or because it suggests Mary Magdalene, bending to wash the feet of Jesus? Or is it simply a memory of Chloe Kiel, the woman who, Dylan claims in his sly, superb 2004 memoir, *Chronicles*, once offered to decorate his shoes – and with whom and her lover, Ray Gooch, he did indeed live for a while, scouring the books on their shelves?

"All the people I used to know/ Are illusions to me now," Dylan sings, wondering at the things time does. He once said that every line in "A Hard Rain's A Gonna Fall" was the first line of a song he'd never have the time to write. "Tangled Up In Blue" seems to be a song about everyone he's ever met, everyone he ever was.

In the New York recording, some have gone on to become "doctor's wives." As released, the line has changed to "carpenter's wives," and that single word throws the song onto another level. You sense the shade of the carpenter's wife in the ancient ballad "Housecarpenter," of which Dylan made a bleak recording in 1962, who abandons her husband to go to Hell with her demon lover. You hear Johnny Cash nailing the truth of "If I Was a Carpenter" in his duet with June

Carter. You glimpse a vision of a Jesus who rejected the mantle of messiah to marry and fade out from history. And, just maybe, you remember the family name Zimmerman derives from "zimmermann," German for "carpenter."

"Tangled Up In Blue" is a song that never ends. Then, when it does end, it's followed by "Simple Twist of Fate," which is "Tangled Up In Blue" all over again.

It repeats that Raeben-inspired method, blurring third- and first-person, distance and intimacy, past and present. It takes place within an Edward Hopperish noir landscape, all neon signs, beat-up hotels, a far-off saxophone echoing across the city night, and waterfront docks (perhaps a reference to Dylan's first great New York love, Suze Rotolo, who once went sailing away from him). But again it is told through language that drips antiquity, *"'twas then he felt alone..."*

This time, though, the song is far simpler, the focus tightened till it fixes with laser intensity on the story of a single moment, the too-brief encounter between a man and the woman he was born to be with, but, for whatever reason, could not be. The moment when she looked at him and he felt *"a spark tingle to his bones."* The moment he feels slipping further and further away from him down the stream of time. The moment he wants back again.

One of the album's surviving New York recordings, you hear clearly here just how intimate, how naked was Dylan's singing across those sessions. There's absolutely no emotional distance between the singer and the song. On the penultimate line of each stanza, the warmth in his voice gets suddenly ripped apart by this howl of anguish, stretching out the shapes of words until they mean more than they mean. Dylan's singing here is so extraordinary, a Sinatra equivalent, that you barely notice the song contains one of the lamest rhymes he ever wrote (*"He hears the ticking of the clocks/ And walks along with a parrot that talks..."*).

There's not a single lyrical slip on the next track, "You're A Big Girl Now," even though Dylan plays a perilous game with it, dealing in cliché throughout. In contrast to the straight-faced platitudes of certain songs on *Nashville Skyline*, however, clichés are here invoked only to be transformed.

Here, time doesn't simply fly: *"Time is a jet plane, it moves too fast,"* like the uncatchable jet plane that took the singer's lover away in Gordon Lightfoot's "Early Mornin' Rain," a song Dylan covered on *Self Portrait*. *"But what a shame,"* he goes on, transfixed, appalled at how one second of now wipes out all of yesterday, *"if all we've shared can't last."*

With its passing nod back to "Just Like a Woman," the song's title sounds like a commonplace, something overheard in the street, but this gloriously lovelorn lament pulls the apparent condescension of the phrase inside out, and aims it back at the speaker. Once again, he's left stranded on the far side of a relationship that has failed, gazing on in wonder as his lover, who always knew that *"love is so simple"* somehow simply moves on, to love again, *"in somebody's room."* She's a big girl now. He breaks just like a little boy, left behind, nursing his crippling pain, not wanting to learn how to deal with it.

"I'm back in the rain, oh, oh/ And you are on dry land..." as he sings it on the album, Dylan makes those mournful "*oh*"s a drowning scream, the size of night. Still, this is one instance where the released

recording is *eclipsed* by the original New York cut. For all its splendours, the album version, with its many guitars, ticking high-hat and stumbling bass, sounds overly busy when compared with the New York take.

The sound of a sad and lonely 3AM, with Dylan's gorgeously resigned vocal, guitar and mourning harmonica set against the distant pining of Buddy Cage's pedal steel and Paul Griffin's glimmering organ, the New York "You're A Big Girl Now" sustains a beautiful tension, so fragile it almost breaks apart, but never quite does.

Then, everything is broken. On "Idiot Wind," the song that comes vomiting out from *"Someone's got in in for me / They're planting stories in the press,"* all the bruised emotions, the chronic sense of the way time wears on, the suspicion of betrayal, the pain, frustration and the held-off hate gusting through *Blood On The Tracks* suddenly whips into a hurricane.

A hate-hymn, a psalm of justified paranoia, "Idiot Wind" begins as the bastard adult child of Dylan's great 1960s put-down anthems, "Like a Rolling Stone" and "Positively 4th Street." Its narrator is besieged by the world, confronted everywhere – in the press, in the street, in his house – by people who relate to him not as who he is, but as who they think he should be: *"Their minds are filled with big ideas, images and distorted facts..."* The lightest it gets is a shrugging joke of deepest black: *"They say I shot a man named Gray/ And took his wife to Italy/ She inherited a million bucks/ And when she died it came to me/ I can't help it if I'm lucky..."*

What has set his horror raging, however, is the realisation that even his love, the "sweet lady" with whom he thought he'd found shelter, has no idea who he is either. (Something he realised

when she asked him "where it was at";
presumably, still not with the diplomat
who carried on his shoulder a Siamese
cat). When he looks up from their
relationship, he finds the fissioning force
of their separation has derailed all
America. Everywhere around are fatal
accidents, blood, war, fire, flies,
crucifixion, lightning. Even the Grand
Coulee Dam, the man-made wonder
Woody Guthrie once eulogised, has been
tainted by it. At the Capitol, the air turns
sour from Nixon's disgrace. Elemental
forces, gravity and destiny, are in motion,
the universe is out of whack, *everything's a
little upside down.* Hell's above, heaven's
below. *The wheels have stopped...*

And it all comes back to her. The
uselessness of their relationship, its failure
to save him from all the empty fury out
there. His disgust has grown so intense
that when she talks, all he can focus on is
her teeth moving, the pointless breath

expelled into the world. She makes him wish he were someone else, that she were dead. In two lines of this song, Dylan pushes *Blood On The Tracks'* experiment with time to a stunning conclusion. Time collapses, moments collide, tomorrow wipes out today and they're already both dead and gone: *"Idiot wind, blowing through the flowers of your tomb/ Blowing through the curtains in your room..."*

The triumph of "Idiot Wind," however, lies in its final lines, when the protagonist's focus widens, suddenly zooms back from his own Lear-like rage, to take in his own culpability. Anger gives way to sorrow, he shifts from mourning that she'll never realise his pain, to acknowledging he'll never understand hers, that he's an idiot, too.

For anyone looing for autobiography, the changes Dylan made to this song between New York and Minneapolis are tantalising. In the earlier version he talks of throwing the I-Ching (a detail that might send some listeners scurrying to explore the hexagram suggested on the album sleeve); admits he and his lover "*pushed each other a little too far*"; reveals his contemptuous awareness at how "*behind my back... imitators steal me blind.*"

Simply bass, guitar and an organ that ripples up under the chorus, barely there at all, the New York "Idiot Wind" is a subdued, tender ache, a compassionate caress of regret that surrounds you like a silver cloud. In a direct comparison, the released version sounds overdone. Where the organ on the first recording sounds the result of a breeze blowing across the keys of a church instrument, the album version is slashed by furious, white-fingered stabs, played by Dylan himself with all the jagged gothic grandeur of a lonely and betrayed Phantom of the Opera (Lon Chaney, not Andrew Lloyd Webber). He turns the word "idiot" into a blue-yodel howl, Jimmy Rodgers via Allen Ginsberg. But, in the context of the album, this soaring, swirling, spew of fury is exactly right, and it comes at exactly the right point. This "Idiot Wind" lays waste to the landscape around it.

In its wake, "Youre Gonna Make Me Lonesome When You Go"" offers a reprieve, breathing space as the LP reaches the end of side one. A New York take, bass, guitar harmonica and this beguilingly coy and soaring, freewheelin' voice, it paints a picture of an easy, idyllic affair, one that sets the countryside blooming like a Disney cartoon, sung by a man less in love with a particular person than in love with love itself, but bright and daffy enough to bend "Honolulu" till it rhymes with "Ashtabula," just to make whoever he's singing to smile. (Ellen Bernstein was born in Ashtabula.) As the titular refrain makes clear, however, even as he's singing their love, he knows it's over.

Blood on the Tracks
and its Shadow:
Side Two

Side two begins like a new morning, but one marked by hail, and one on which the sun refuses to shine.

Recorded with Deliverance and overdubbed with Buddy Cage's pedal steel, "Meet Me in the Morning" is an electric blues, expertly constructed from elements worn smooth by countless blues before. The narrator, the victim of a careless lover, walks a lightless landscape watched by animals who have observed thousands like him in songs before down the years. He's outrun hound dogs; he's heard the little rooster crowing, the same rooster Willie Dixon lost to the Rolling Stones, or the crowing cock who chimed out St Peter's betrayal of Christ. The cosmos is stained in sympathy for his helpless love: *"Look at the sun sinkin' like a ship/ Ain't that just like my heart, babe/ When you kiss my lips?"*

Fine as it is, however, the inclusion of "Meet Me in the Morning" on the album at the expense of its near-identical New York soundalike, "Call Letter Blues" seems evidence of Dylan's attempt to wipe out his autobiographical tracks.

The latter, one of the most raw and desperately personal blues he has ever written, is a song of a higher, deeper order. Haunted by the eternal sound of tolling bells, its abandoned protagonist wanders the planet searching the faces of passing strangers, *"in case I might see you."*

At once bitterly betrayed, and achingly alone, he tries to juggle boiling anger and helplessness with the need to still deal with the polite enquiries of mutual acquaintances (*"when your friends come by for you, I dunno what to say"*), come-ons from willing women, and the uncomprehending wails of his kids: *"The children cry for mother/ I tell 'em mother took a trip."* Unleashing the most vicious vocal he's ever recorded, Dylan spits out that "*trip*" with a distaste that leaves you aghast, wondering what hellish kind of degraded, deluded adventure the missing woman has gone chasing.

At the climax, Cage lets rip with a ferocious, but precise, easy scream of a solo, scorching the earth, like the Velvet Underground's Sterling Morrison gone country.

Blood On The Tracks reaches a turning point with "Lily, Rosemary and the Jack of Hearts." Unlike any other song on the record, this rambling, unspooling ballad is presented as a pure fiction. It strikes a glaring note at first, but it functions like the play within the play in *Hamlet*, presenting the same story to us, in a different way.

A pulp-Western fantasy, set in some muddy Deadwood of a place, populated by ciphers as thin as playing-cards, all of them reflections of each other, it's as if the narrator has fallen asleep, mind swimming, and his brain has ordered his thoughts into this fictional construct to make sense of them.

His dream becomes a fantasy of how it should have been, as he casts himself as the roguish outlaw hero who looks "like a saint," the guy all men want to be like, and all women would kill to be with, but who can never be tied down. The desperate, breakneck, almost slapstick clatter of the released Minneapolis version – unbelievably, the first take of the song – emphasises its air of unreality, with its oompah bass, skipping organ and Dylan blowing frantically on a harmonica that's in an entirely different key.

After this fable, the album wakes again, and sighs. "If You See Her, Say Hello," is another song written one late night alone on the wrong side of a bitter separation. The singer casts his mind out to his wandering lover – she might be as far away as Tangier, the mythic retreat where all the artists go – trying to keep his cool, keep casual, keep a close watch on his feelings, but unable to stop resentment and hurt bursting out: *"Tell her she can look me up/ If she's got the time."*

Again, in its journey from New York to Minneapolis, the song has been altered. Lyrically, Dylan sands down the edges of emotionally ragged lines. The original *"If you're making love to her…"* becomes instead, *"If you get close to her…"* Similarly, the released album performance has an air of detachment when contrasted with the exquisitely naked New York original, one of those tracks on which you can hear

Dylan's jacket buttons hitting against his guitar.

And yet, in this song that is about separation, distance and time, the balance Dylan strikes between intimacy and detachment, between being up close and far away, is rather perfect. This released version is to be cherished, anyway, if only for the closing banks of mandolins, which make a sound like memory itself.

That memory becomes the memory of "Shelter From the Storm." "Deceptively simple" hardly sums up this three-chord New York evocation of a lost, but eternally sought love. Once more, the song sees a world made up from timeless elements, and battered by time. A muddy universe in which *"newborn babies"* and *"old men with broken teeth"* alike are left stranded and wailing, where *"nothing really matters much, it's doom alone that counts,"* where it's *"hopeless and forlorn"* – but where, when you catch it, love offers a salvation so powerful that it's worth forever searching for. No matter that it's doomed never to last.

When the narrator recalls being lost in a period *"when blackness was a virtue,"* when he was *"burned out... buried... poisoned... blown out... hunted...,"* and how a woman offered him the rescue of her simple, divine love, you might think of the speeding acid-hipster Dylan of the '60s, and you might think about his retreat into the Woodstock silence.

Like "Meet Me in the Morning" it's another song that has taken the place on the album of an almost exact soundalike from the New York sessions, in this case "Up To Me," in which Dylan had sketched a quick self-portrait *"...my lone guitar... the harmonica around my neck... no one else could play that tune..."*

"Shelter From the Storm," however, has such a simple potency that it burns into irrelevancy all questions of whether it's about Bob Dylan, Sara Lownds, Suze Rotolo or Ellen Bernstein. Like all of *Blood On The Tracks*, it belongs to anyone who's ever been in love, whether for ten years, or 25, or a single day. (Or even, given how noir movies tend to lodge in Dylan's imagination, a single stolen afternoon, like the one Humphrey Bogart shares with the bookshop girl who literally offers him shelter from a storm in *The Big Sleep*.)

The last breath of the storm passes, and all that's left is "Buckets of Rain." There's a barely-noticed glory to this final song, layers of resonance and reference, despite its simplicity. Dylan's lazy-busy fingerpicking and the soft sad mischief of his burring, purring vocal invoke the gentle spirit of the bluesman Mississippi John Hurt. The melody takes Tom Paxton's "Bottle of Wine" and introduces it to a faint memory of the melody of Mungo Jerry's "In the Summertime" (a song Dylan would unleash unlikely covers of during concerts in the 1980s).

He sings *"Little red wagon/ Little red bike,"* and you might see abandoned children's toys, left out in the rain by a lonely farmhouse until the kids come to visit again. But Dylan is playing with the old New Orleans expression "that's your red wagon," which means, more or less, "it's your business," fitting the song's prevailing mood of accepting how things just go they way they go, and there isn't much can be done about it.

("*I was in love with you baby/ You was in love with some other man,*" Arthur "Big Boy" Crudup sang in 1945, "*Now that's your red wagon/ You can roll it along/ When you leave me this time/ Some other woman's got your home...*")

The opening lines – *"Buckets of Rain/ Buckets of Tears/ Got all them buckets comin' out of my ears"* - sets the song up as an absurdist nursery rhyme, but it's one that comes from a place of hard-won wisdom. Finally, the narrator seems ready to settle for his unchanging place in the stream of time. Is there a much better summary of human behaviour and the way life works than the lines, *"I been meek/ And hard like an oak/ I seen pretty people disappear like smoke/ Friends will arrive, friends will disappear"*?

Actually, yes, there is. This chiming, humming little Zen-blues ends with another, more perfect yet: *"Life is sad/ Life is a bust/ All ya can do is do what you must/ You do what you must do and ya do it well/ I do it for you, honey baby/ Can't you tell?"*

Blood On The Tracks ends with Dylan picking out the final notes of this little song of misery and acquiescence, wistful and warm. If you really listen, though, you notice something else, too. You hear just how hard he's picking those sharp steel guitar strings. Playing with furiously focused calm. Like he'll lose it if he stops. Playing so hard the strings sound as if they're almost snapping, cutting into his fingers. Like he's about to start bleeding all over again.

After the Rain
The Blood Legacy, from Then until Now

"A lot of people tell me they enjoyed that album," Dylan snapped at folksinger Mary Travers when she told him exactly that during an uncomfortable radio interview in March, 1975. "It's hard for me to relate to that - I mean, people *enjoying* that type of pain..."

Travers wasn't alone. Rendering the specific universal, *Blood On The Tracks* saw Dylan's concerns dovetail with currents in the air like they hadn't for years. Without being specifically about 1974 -1975, it caught a haunted mood as perfectly as that year's stunning noir *Chinatown*, a movie which similarly shuffled wistful nostalgia and romance with bleakness and harsh, clear-eyed disenchantment. Rocketing to number one in America, it garnered the most laudatory reviews of any Dylan album since 1968.

There were dissenting voices, notably *Rolling Stone*'s Jon Landau, who spent his bizarre, grudgingly faintly-positive notice explaining why Charlie Chaplin was better than Dylan, and positing that Dylan had made "no single record to equal... Martha and the Vandellas' 'Heat Wave.'" Most of the negative remarks focused on the playing on the album. Landau felt, "the accompanying musicians have never sounded more indifferent."

Indeed, all through the record, you can hear dodgy notes, chords not-quite formed. But those imperfections, that raw feeling, are this album's vital, expressionistic, stuff. Criticising *Blood On The Tracks* because Dylan allows you to hear missed notes is like criticising Van Gogh's *Wheatfield With Crows* because he hasn't painted the birds' plumage in a photorealistic manner.

More important than its critical reception, *Blood On The Tracks* set Dylan raging again. The torrent unleashed carried him on through into his next album, *Desire*, and its attendant tour, The Rolling Thunder Review, those extraordinary concerts during which, galvanised by the strength, heat and light of his new material, Dylan was inspired to attack his old catalogue with renewed vigour.

Simultaneously, he continued to apply the painterly, time-defying, shifting-perspective method opened up by his exposure to Norman Raeben. It inspired the whole style of that tour's singular, lambasted filmic record, *Renaldo and Clara*, and, in Dylan's own estimation, reached a zenith with the songs he wrote for 1978's much-neglected *Street Legal* album.

Blood On The Tracks shouldn't be considered "Dylan's divorce record" for one simple reason: it wasn't made at the time of his divorce. Whether or not they were specifically brought back together by the devastating emotional candour of the record, by mid-1975, Dylan and Sara were a couple again. By mid-1977, though, they were divorced, and involved in one of the most noxiously bitter custody battles ever fought in the American courts. "I can't go home without fear for my safety," Sara stated in an application for a restraining order against Dylan, published in several press outlets at the time. "I was in such fear of him that I locked doors in the home to protect myself from his violent outbursts and temper tantrums..."

Stemming from *Blood On The Tracks'* sense of abandoned yearning, however, the albums of Dylan's mid-1970s renaissance do lay out a metaphorical parallel to his and Sara's dissolution. *Desire* feels like the reconciliation, the wild, magical Indian-summer of a love that was simply meant to be, and couldn't be denied. *Street Legal*, on which Dylan's old "thin, wild mercury sound" was transmuted into savage back gold, is the sound of what comes after the bitter end, of someone picking himself back up, seeing the world as strange, and moving on again.

For those seeking genuinely autobiographical songs, however, the unholy grail must be the rumoured book of never-recorded, never-repeated songs Dylan reportedly wrote and played to friends in private around the time of his real divorce. Apparently dark and poisonous compositions, among them, the song title "I'm Cold" was about as light as it got.

By the end of *Street Legal*, Dylan had reached the end of the road *Blood On The Tracks* had opened up to him. It would take God Himself to move him along toward his next stage – but that's another story.

When he did get back on track, though, he found *Blood On The Tracks* still waiting for him. Whether as something to escape, or to re-interrogate, the album has proved endlessly renewing for Dylan. The keynote song, "Tangled Up In Blue," in particular has never stopped evolving in concert. In 1978, as Dylan entered his Gospel period, the lyrics shifted so that the narrator no longer frequented topless bars, and the book of Italian poetry disappeared, to be literally replaced by a Bible. He wouldn't play the song again until 1984, unveiling an almost entirely rewritten version during that year's London show, yet another "comeback," preserved on the *Real Live* album.

Across the "Never Ending Tour" of the 1980s and early 90s, the song changed guises constantly. By 2000, it had shifted again, back towards its old self lyrically (meanwhile, the girl in "If You See Her, Say Hello" had dyed her hair blue), while, musically, it had been transformed into a guitar-sparring acoustic hoedown, reminiscent of a backwoods version of Television, trying to remember how to play "Sweet Home Alabama."

On his extraordinary European tour of 2013, Dylan, 72 and still out there moving on the road, delivered a set almost fully focussed on his most recent songs, the remarkable modernist 21st-century-collage blues of *"Love And Theft,"* *Modern Times, Together Through Life* and *Tempest.* Amid those new songs, however, he sat at his grand piano and revisited, revised, and edited "Tangled Up In Blue" and "Simple Twist Of Fate," yet again, the latter now emerging as an exquisite, slow-soft shuffling reading, in which the narrator now found a note left on his pillow by object of his desire, *"What it say? It said: 'You shoulda met me back in '58...'"*

He holds the songs up still, still up close, and then at arm's length, turning them, examining them, looking for something new, or searching for something very old.

Meanwhile, listeners continue to look for Dylan himself in there. During that Mary Travers radio interview in 1975, he blew the lid off the question of whether *Blood On The Tracks* might be read autobiographically: *"It's hard for me to relate to... people enjoying that type of pain."* But he's been trying to put it back on ever since.

In 1985, the writer Bill Flanagan asked Dylan if he felt he had ever put something in a song that was too personal. "I came pretty close with that song 'Idiot Wind,'" Dylan replied, before diving for cover. "I didn't feel that one was too personal, but I felt it *seemed* too personal. Which might be the same thing, I don't know..."

Dylan doesn't mention *Blood On The Tracks* by name in the first volume of his *Chronicles*. But he does say: "Eventually I would even record an entire album based on Chekhov short stories – critics thought it was autobiographical, that was fine."

Is that *Blood On The Tracks* he's talking about? Well, there are all those horses and uniforms and fields in there... Then again, as a Chekhov fan, Dylan would be familiar with this passage from the great author's uncanny, unsettling story, "The Black Monk":

"He knew from experience that the best cure for shattered nerves is work. One should sit down at a table and force oneself at all costs to concentrate on one idea, no matter what."

That sounds like a fair description of the making of this album that does not let go. As Dylan sneered in 1966's abandoned "She's Your Lover Now," a song he never recorded to his satisfaction, *"Pain sure brings out the best in people, doesn't it?"* In 1997's gorgeous "Not Dark Yet," he reiterated the point: *"Behind every beautiful thing, there's been some kind of pain."*

And behind some beautiful things, there's every kind of pain. But, sometimes, it's the beauty that endures.

Bibliography and Sources

- Chekhov, Anton: *The Black Monk*, 1894
- Cott, Jonathan: *Rolling Stone* interview with Dylan, January 1978
- Crowe, Cameron: interview for the liner notes of *Biograph*, Columbia Records, 1985
- Dylan, Bob: *Chronicles, Volume 1*, Simon & Schuster, 2004
- Flanagan, Bill: interview in *Written In My Soul: Conversations with Rock's Great Songwriters*, Contemporary Books, 1986
- Oppel, Pete: interview for The Dallas Morning News, November 1978
- Preston, John: interview for *The Sunday Telegraph*, September 2004

- Shelton, Robert: *No Direction Home – The Life and Music of Bob Dylan*, Beech Tree Books/ William Morrow, 1986
- Saal, Hubert: interview for *Newsweek*, January 1968
- Sounes, Howard: *Down the Highway – The Life of Bob Dylan*, Grove, 2001